博古通今学汉语丛书
Gems of the Chinese Language Through the Ages

成语 101
101 Common Chinese Idioms and Set Phrases

By Binyong YIN
Translated by Hui HAN

华语教学出版社 · 伦敦
Sinolingua · London

101 Common Chinese Idioms and Set Phrases
Compiled by Binyong YIN
Translated by Hui HAN

Editor: Xiaolin LIU
Cover design: Shaowen TANG
Illustration: Feng LIU, Gengtao LIU

Copyright ©2012 by Sinolingua London Ltd.
First published in Great Britain in January 2012 by **Sinolingua London Ltd.**

Unit 13, Park Royal Metro Centre
Britannia Way
London NW10 7PA
Tel: +44(0)2089519305
Fax: +44(0)2084530709
Email: editor@cypressbooks.com

Distributed by Cypress Book Co. (UK) Ltd.
Tel: +44(0)2084530687
Fax: +44(0)2084530709
Email: sales@cypressbooks.com
Website: www.cypressbooks.com

Printed in China

ISBN 978-1-907838-22-4

Preface

What comes next for a student of the Chinese as the second language after mastering its phonetics, grammar, and most of its vocabulary? The next highly desirable step would be to study some of the more typical Chinese expressions—such as its idioms and set phrases, two-part allegorical sayings, or even its classical poetry. These expressions are so closely related to the Chinese language and Chinese culture that once one has mastered them, one will not only be able to speak idiomatic Chinese and sound more like a native speaker, but will also be able to penetrate deeper into Chinese culture and gradually become a "China Hand".

For this purpose, we have compiled this series Gems of the Chinese Language Through the Ages which comprises the following five titles:

101 Common Chinese Idioms and Set Phrases

101 Pearls of Chinese Wisdom

101 Chinese Two-Part Allegorical Sayings

The Stories Behind 101 Chinese Idioms

101 Ancient Chinese Poems

These idioms and sayings have been chosen for the frequency with which they are used, their practical value and their expressiveness. Each is accompanied by an English translation and an illustration. Some of the more obscure expressions have been further annotated in both Chinese and English. A CD in MP3 format is provided for each book.

前　言

　　学习汉语的外国学生，当他们初步掌握了汉语的语音、词汇、语法和文字时，很想进一步提高自己的汉语水平。怎样提高呢？一件重要的事就是需要掌握一些汉语语言中最有特色的东西——例如成语、谚语、歇后语、典故和古诗。这些东西既和汉语汉字有密切关系，又和中华民族的文化背景有密切关系。掌握了它们，不但能够丰富外国人汉语的表达能力，而且也能够增强他们汉语表达的本土特色。简而言之，他们所掌握的汉语就更像汉语了。这就向成为一个"中国通"迈出了重要的一步。

　　为以上目的，我们给这样的外国学生编了一套"博古通今学汉语丛书"，包括"成语101"、"谚语101"、"歇后语101"、"典故101"和"古诗101"。

　　本套书精选汉语中最有价值的、常用的、表现力强的成语、谚语、歇后语、典故和古诗各101则。每则均附英文释义，每则配一幅精美插图，另有一些难解词语中英文注释。随书附MP3光盘。

目　录
Contents

成语 101

101 Common Chinese Idioms and Set Phrases

Àntú-suǒjì

1. 按图索骥

Looking for a fine steed with the aid of its picture

春秋时代（公元前 770—公元前 476），秦国有个识马的能手，大家叫他"伯乐"。他把识别马的知识和经验写成了一本书，还在书上配合文字画出了各种好马的形态。而他的儿子一点也不懂得识马的知识，只凭着书上画的图像去寻找好马，找来找去，一匹好马也没有找到。

"按图索骥^①"这个成语用来比喻没有实践经验、只知道机械地按老规矩办事。

In the Spring and Autumn Period (770-476 BC), there was a man in the State of Qin called Bo Le, who was an expert at judging horses. Based on his experience and knowledge of horses, he wrote a book in which he introduced the characterisitcs of fine horses both in words and illustrations. His son, having no first-hand experience of horses, set out to look for fine horses according to the illustration in the book. However, he could not find any.

This idiom is used metaphorically to describe someone lacking practical experience and doing things mechanically by following set rules.

---

① 骥：好马。(fine horse)

Bǎifā-bǎizhòng

2. 百发百中

A hundred shots, a hundred bullseyes

　　春秋时代，楚国有个人叫养由基，他射箭的技术非常高超。有人在柳树上选择了高低不同的三片叶子，分别注上"一"、"二"、"三"的记号。养由基站在百步以外的地方，拉开弓，搭上箭，果然第一箭射中"一"叶，第二箭射中"二"叶，第三箭射中"三"叶，<u>丝毫不差</u>。

　　"百发百中"这个成语，形容射箭技术高超，每次都能命中。以后常常用来比喻做事有充分的把握，总能达到预期的目的。

In the Spring and Autumn Period, there was an excellent archer in the State of Chu called Yang Youji. To test his skill, someone chose three leaves at different heights on a willow tree, and challenged him to hit them all, one after another. Yang Youji stood more than one hundred paces away and hit the three leaves in three shots.

This idiom describes excellent marksmanship. Later it became used to refer to great precision and perfect assurance.

Bānmén-nòngfǔ

3. 班门弄斧

Showing off one's proficiency with the axe before Lu Ban the master carpenter

　　古代有一个建筑和雕刻技术非常高超的人，名叫鲁班，木匠行里尊称他为祖师。传说他曾用木头制作了一只五彩斑斓（bānlán）的凤凰，能够在空中飞翔（xiáng）三天不掉下来。在鲁班门前摆弄斧子，当然显得有些自不量力了。

　　"班门弄斧"这个成语，用来比喻在行家面前显示本领。

Lu Ban was supposed to be a consummate carpenter in ancient times and regarded the master of carpentry. It is said that he once carved a wooden phoenix that was so lifelike that it actually flew in the sky for three days. Thus it was considered the height of folly to show off one's skill with an axe in front of Lu Ban.

This idiom excoriates those who show off their slight accomplishments in front of experts.

Bēigōng-shéyǐng

4. 杯弓蛇影

Mistaking the reflection of a bow for a snake

晋朝（公元 265—420）时，有一个叫乐广的人，请他的朋友到家里喝酒。朋友端起酒杯喝酒的时候，忽然看见杯子里面有条小蛇的影子，他当时勉强将酒喝下，但回家后总是想起这件令人恶心的事，以至于生了病。乐广知道后，就把朋友再次请来，还是坐在原来的地方喝酒。那位朋友这才弄明白了，原来杯中的蛇影，是墙上挂着的一张弓映照出来的。事情弄明白了，病也就好了。

这个成语比喻疑神疑鬼，自相惊扰。

In the Jin Dynasty (265-420), a man called Yue Guang once invited a friend to have a drink at his home. When the friend lifted his cup, he saw a small snake in the wine, yet he still forced himself to drink it. Back home, the friend couldn't get the incident off his mind, and felt so disgusted that he fell ill. Hearing about this, Yue Guang invited his friend to his home again. He asked him to sit in the same place and drink. When his friend sat down, he saw that the image of the snake in the cup was actually the reflection of a bow hung on the wall. Realizing this, his friend recovered quickly from his illness.

This idiom describes a condition of being overly suspicious and thus bringing trouble upon oneself.

Bìmén-zàochē

5. 闭门造车

Building a cart behind closed doors

古时候，有一个人想造一辆很精巧的车子。他不去学习别人制造车子的实际经验，却把自己关在家里冥（míng）思苦想。费了很多工夫，车子虽然造好了，但是推出去却不能使用。

这个成语比喻只凭主观想象办事，不顾客观实际，结果总是碰壁。

In ancient times, there was a man who wanted to make a fine chariot. But, instead of learning how to make one from experts, he shut himself up at home and worked on it alone. Despite the time and effort he spent on it, the chariot was useless.

This idiom is used metaphorically to mean being too subjective and disregarding the rest of the world.

Bìngrù-gāohuāng

6. 病入膏肓

The disease has attacked the vital organs

春秋时候，晋景公生了病。病中梦见自己的疾病变成两个小人在他旁边谈话。一个说："我害怕医生会伤害我们。"另一个说："不要怕，我们躲到肓①的上面,膏②的下面,医生能把我们怎样！"第二天，医生来给他诊断病情时说："你的病没法子治啦！病在肓的上面，膏的下面，药剂的效力无法到达了。"

这个成语比喻事情已经非常严重，到了不可挽救的程度。

In the Spring and Autumn Period, Duke Jing of the State of Jin fell ill. One night he dreamed that his disease had turned into two small figures who were talking beside him. One said, "I'm afraid the doctor will hurt us." The other said, "Don't worry. We can hide above *huang* and below *gao*. Then the doctor will not be able to do anything to us." The next day, having examined the duke, the doctor said, "I am afraid your disease is incurable, Your Majesty. It's above *huang* and below *gao*, where no medicine can reach."

This idiom refers to a hopeless condition.

---

① 肓：心脏和膈膜之间。(the area between the heart and the diaphragm)

② 膏：心尖脂肪。(fat around the heart)

Cǎomù-jiēbīng

7. 草木皆 ① 兵

Every bush and tree looks like an enemy

---

① 皆：都是。(all)

公元 383 年，前秦国王苻坚带了 80 万大军攻打东晋，在淝水一带，被晋朝大将谢玄的前锋部队打得大败。苻坚登上寿阳城，看见晋军阵容严整，心里害怕起来。再远望八公山上长着许多草和树木，也以为是东晋的士兵，更加惊恐万分。后来苻坚全军覆没（fùmò），带着少数残余的队伍逃了回去。

这个成语用来形容人在极度惊恐时，疑神疑鬼的心理状态。

In 383 AD, the King of Former Qin period, Fu Jian, led a huge army to attack Eastern Jin. After losing the first round of fighting, Fu Jian looked down from a city wall, and was terrified when he saw the formidable battle array of the Eastern Jin army. He then looked at the mountains around and mistook the grass and the trees for enemy soldiers. As a result, when the nervous Fu Jian led his army into battle, it suffered a crushing defeat.

This idiom describes how one can defeat oneself by imagining difficulties where no difficulties exist.

Chuīmáo-qiúcī
8. 吹毛求疵 ①

Blow apart the hairs upon a fur to discover any defects

---

① 疵：毛病。(fault, defect)

　　古时候，有一个专门喜欢寻找小毛病的人。有一次他到商店里去买兽皮。为了检查这张兽皮是不是一张好皮，就吹开兽皮上面的毛，一处一处地寻找里面的小毛病。

　　后来人们用这个成语比喻故意挑剔（tī）毛病，寻找差错。

In ancient times there was a man who was a notorious nitpicker. Once, he went to buy a fur cloak. To check the fur, he blew the hairs apart, looking for any trivial defects.

This idiom came to be used to describe the act of deliberately looking for tiny faults.

Dǎcǎo-jīngshé

9. 打草惊蛇

Beating the grass and flushing out the snake

古时候有一个县官，贪污受贿（huì），谋取私利。有一次，有人写了一个状子，控告他的秘书贪污受贿。这个县官一边看状子，一边直打寒颤（zhàn）。他在状子后面写了八个字：“汝（rǔ）虽打草，吾已惊蛇。”（“你虽然打的是地上的草，但我就像伏在草里面的蛇，已经受到惊吓了。”）

这个成语比喻做机密的事行动不小心，使对方觉察后有所防备。

In ancient times there was a county magistrate who took bribes and practised graft. One day, somebody sent him a petition accusing his secretary of practising graft and taking bribes. The magistrate trembled when he read the petition and wrote on it, "You have beaten the grass and frightened a snake," implying that he was the snake lurking in the grass.

This idiom refers to alerting the target of one's scheme through incautious action.

Diàohǔ-líshān

10. 调虎离山

Luring the tiger out of the mountains

老虎是居住在深山里的凶猛野兽。如果用计策引诱老虎离开了深山，人们就比较容易制服它了。

"调虎离山"这个成语，常常用来比喻使用计策，引诱人离开有利的环境，以便于控制或消灭他们。

The tiger is a ferocious animal which lives in the mountains. Only by luring it away from the mountains can one subdue it.

This idiom is used metaphorically to mean enticing a rival out of his comfort zone in order to put him at a disadvantage.

Dōngshī-xiàopín
11. 东施效颦 [1]

Aping the beauty's frown

---

[1] 颦：皱眉。 (to knit one's brows)

春秋时代，越国有个美女叫做西施。西施有胸口痛的病，病发作的时候，她会捧着胸口，皱着眉头。村子里有一个丑女子，叫做东施，她觉得这个姿态很美，于是也学西施的样子捧着胸口、皱着眉头走路。她自己以为很美，其实这样一来却更显得丑了，连行人看见了都躲得远远的。

后来人们用"东施效颦"这个成语比喻不恰当的模仿，带来相反的效果。

In the Spring and Autumn Period, there was a beauty in the State of Yue called Xishi. She frequently suffered from pains in her chest, so she would often double over and knit her brows in pain. There was an ugly girl in the village called Dongshi who envied Xishi. Striving to emulate Xishi, she imitated her stoop, knitting her brows at the same time. She thought that this made her elegant, but in fact it only made her more ugly.

Later, this idiom came to be used to describe improper imitations that produce an effect that is opposite to what is intended.

Duìniú-tánqín

12. 对牛弹琴

Playing the lute to a cow

古时候，有一个人琴弹得很好。一次，他对着牛弹了一段曲子，希望牛也来欣赏他的技巧。曲子虽然很好听，但是牛却丝毫不理会，只顾埋头吃草。这个人没法，只好摇摇头叹了口气。

"对牛弹琴"这个成语，比喻对不懂道理的人讲道理。也用来讥笑说话的人不看对象。

In ancient times there was a man who played the lute very well. Once, he played a tune in front of a cow, hoping that the cow would appreciate it. The tune was melodious, but the cow showed no reaction and just kept on eating grass. The man sighed and went away.

This idiom is used to describe situations where someone is reasoning with stubborn people or talking to the wrong audience.

Fùjīng-qǐngzuì
13. 负荆^① 请罪

Bringing the birch and asking for a flogging

---

① 荆：一种灌木的枝条。(bramble branch)

战国（公元前 475—公元前 221）时，廉（lián）颇和蔺（lìn）相如同在赵国作官。蔺相如立了大功，被封为上卿（qīng），官位比廉颇大。廉颇不服气，扬言要当面羞辱蔺相如。蔺相如为了国家的利益，处处避让，不与他相斗。后来廉颇认识到自己的错误，感到十分惭愧，便脱掉上衣，背上荆条，到蔺相如家里当面请罪。

"负荆请罪"这个成语用来表示向别人赔礼、认错。

In the Warring States Period (475-221 BC), Lian Po and Lin Xiangru were both officials of the State of Zhao. Having rendered outstanding service, Lin Xiangru was promoted above Lian Po. Disgruntled, Lian Po announced that he intended to humiliate Lin the next time he met him. Lin Xiangru, putting the benefit of the country first, avoided Lian Po in order not to cause conflict. Later, when Lian Po realized his mistake, he was so ashamed that he went to Lin's home carrying bramble branches on his naked back and asked Lin to punish him.

This idiom indicates acknowledging one's mistake and offering a sincere apology for it.

Gōngkuī-yíkuì

14. 功亏一篑 ①

Ruining an enterprise for the lack of one basket

---

① 篑：盛土的筐子。(a basket for carrying earth)

从前有一个人，打算修建一座土台。他辛辛苦苦地挖土、搬土，费了很多工夫。眼看土台快要修建成了，可是到了最后，只差一"篑"（盛土的筐子）土的时候，他不愿意干了。土台最终没有修建好。

"功亏一篑"这个成语被人们用来比喻事情即将完成，却不能坚持到底。含有惋惜的意思。

Once a man planned to build a terrace. He worked very hard and spent a lot of time digging and carrying basketfuls of earth. When the mound was almost completed and only one more basketful of earth was needed, the man gave up and the terrace was never completed.

This idiom means to fail in an enterprise because one doesn't make a final effort. It has a pitying connotation.

Gùbù-zìfēng

15. 故 ① 步自封 ②

Content with staying where one is

---

① 故：旧，从前。(old, before)

② 封：限制在某一范围。(limited within a range)

从前有一个人，想到很远的地方去。可是，他举起步来，总是在老路上转圈子。走啊，走啊，算起来应该已经走了很远的路了，可是一看，还是停留在原来的老地方。

"故步自封"这个成语比喻一个人老是停留在原地，安于现状，不求进取。

Once upon a time, a certain man wanted to go to a distant place. He set off on his journey, but he kept on walking in circles. After a long time, he thought he must have travelled a great distance. However, when he looked around, he found that he was still in the same place he started from.

This idiom is used to describe those who are content with things as they are, and are not eager to make progress.

Hánshā-shèyǐng

16. 含沙射影

Spitting sand on a shadow—attacking someone by insinuation

传说水里面有一种虫，名叫蜮（yù）。它头上有角，背上有甲，没有眼睛，长了三只脚，有翅膀能飞，嘴里有一个像弩（nǔ）一样的东西。如果听见人的脚步声，它就用嘴含着细沙朝人射来，人或者人的影子要是被射中（zhòng）了，就会生病。

"含沙射影"这个成语用来比喻在暗地里对人进行诽谤、中（zhòng）伤。

Legend has it that there was once a water monster called Yu. It had horns, a shell, wings and three feet, but no eyes. There was a catapult in its mouth from which it shot sand. If Yu heard the steps of a man, it would shoot sand from its mouth at him. Even if the man's shadow was hit, the man would fall ill.

This idiom refers to vilifying people by insinuation.

Hújiǎ-hǔwēi

17. 狐假 ① 虎威

Basking in reflected glory

---

① 假：借用。(to borrow)

老虎在山林里捉到了一只狐狸，要吃掉它。狐狸连忙说："你不能吃我，我是天帝派来统治百兽的。你要吃了我，就违抗了天帝的命令。你不信，就跟我到山林里去一趟，看百兽见了我是不是都很害怕。"老虎相信了狐狸的话，就跟在狐狸的后面走进山林。百兽见了果然都纷纷逃命。老虎以为百兽真的害怕狐狸而不知道是害怕自己，于是就把狐狸给放了。

"狐假虎威"这个成语用来比喻倚仗别人的势力去欺压人或吓唬人。

A tiger caught a fox in a forest, and was just about to eat it, when the fox said, "You mustn't eat me. I was sent by Heaven to rule the animals. By eating me, you will violate the command of Heaven. If you don't believe me, just follow me to see whether the animals are afraid of me." The tiger agreed, and followed the fox as it walked around the forest. Upon seeing them, all the animals ran away. The tiger thought they were afraid of the fox, so he let it go. He didn't realize that it was him that the beasts really feared.

This idiom means relying on another's power to bully or frighten others.

Húlún-tūnzǎo

18. 囫囵 ① 吞枣

Gulping down a whole date

---

① 囫囵: 整个儿。(entirely)

有一个医生向人介绍枣子的性能时说："枣子对人的脾脏（pízàng）有益，但是对牙齿有害。"旁边有一个人听了以后就说："我有一个好办法，吃枣子的时候不用牙齿嚼（jiáo），一口吞下去，这样不就可以利用它的益处而避免它的害处了吗？"

以后人们就根据这个故事，把读书或理解事情不加分析、笼统地接受下去的行为叫做"囫囵吞枣"。

A physician once told a group of people, "Dates are good for the spleen, but harmful for the teeth." On hearing this, one man said, "I have a good idea, when eating dates, we should just swallow them whole without chewing them. Then we can both enjoy the advantages and avoid the disadvantages of them."

This story gave rise to the above idiom, which refers to lapping up information without digesting it, or reading without understanding or analyzing the text.

Huàbǐng-chōngjǐ

19. 画饼充饥

Allaying hunger with pictures of cakes

三国时代（公元 220—280）魏国的皇帝曹睿（ruì），准备选拔一个有才能的人到朝廷来做官。曹睿对他的大臣说："选择人才，不能光找有虚名的人。虚名好像是在地上画的一块饼，只能看，不能解决肚子饥饿的问题啊！"

后来人们就用"画饼充饥"这个成语比喻用空想安慰自己，不能解决实际问题。

In the Three Kingdoms Period (220-280), the King of the State of Wei, Cao Rui, wanted to find a very capable man to work for him. He said to his ministers, "When choosing a talented person, always beware of one with a false reputation. A false reputation is just like a picture of a cake painted on the ground; it cannot actually relieve hunger."

Later, this idiom came to be used to mean comforting oneself with unrealistic thoughts and not solving problems.

Huàlóng-diǎnjīng

20. 画龙点睛

Putting the finishing touches on a picture of a dragon

南北朝（公元 420—589）时期，有个画家叫张僧繇（yóu）。有一次，他到一个寺庙去游玩，在墙壁上面画了四条龙，可是都没有画出眼睛。看画的人觉得很奇怪，问他为什么不画出眼睛。他说："眼睛是龙的关键，画上眼睛，龙就会飞走了。"大家不相信他说的话。张僧繇拿起笔来，刚给两条龙点上眼睛，立刻电闪雷鸣，两条龙飞向天空，墙上只剩下两条没有画眼睛的龙。

"画龙点睛"这个成语用来比喻讲话或写文章时，在关键地方加一两句重要的话，使内容更加生动有力。

During the Southern and Northern Dynasties (420-589), there was a painter called Zhang Sengyou. Once he visited a temple and painted on its wall four dragons, but gave none of them eyes. The onlookers felt that this was odd, and asked why he hadn't painted their eyes. He answered, "Eyes are crucial for dragons. If their eyes were painted, the dragons would fly away." Nobody believed this, so Zhang Sengyou took up his brush and added eyes to two of the dragons. No sooner had he finished than the two dragons flew into the sky amid a thunderstorm. Only the two without eyes remained on the wall.

This idiom is used to describe how, when writing or speaking, one or two key sentences will enhance one's words.

Huàshé-tiānzú

21. 画蛇添足

Drawing a snake and adding feet

战国时代有个楚国人祭（jì）他的祖先。仪式结束后，他拿出一壶酒赏给手下的几个人。大家商量说："我们都来画蛇，谁先画好谁就喝这壶酒。"其中有一个人先画好了。但他看到同伴还没有画完，就又给蛇添上了脚。这时，另一个人也画好了，夺过酒壶把酒喝了，并且说："蛇本来是没有脚的，你怎么能给它添上脚呢？"

"画蛇添足"这个成语比喻做了多余而不恰当的事，反而把事情弄糟了。

In the Warring States Period, a man in the State of Chu offered a sacrifice to his ancestors. After the ceremony, the man gave a beaker of wine to his servants. The servants discussed how the wine should be shared and decided that they would each draw a picture of a snake; the one who finished the drawing first would get the wine. One of them drew very rapidly. Seeing that the others were still busy drawing, he added feet to his snake. At that moment another man finished, snatched the beaker and drank the wine, saying, "A snake doesn't have feet. How could you add feet to a snake?"

This idiom refers to ruining a venture by doing unnecessary things.

Jīnggōng-zhīniǎo

22. 惊弓之鸟

Birds startled by the mere twang of a bowstring

战国时期魏国有个名叫更羸（léi）的人。一天，他对国王说："我只要拉开弓，空射一下，就能把天上的鸟射下来。"国王不相信。更羸便对准天上飞来的一只雁射去，果真那只雁听到拉弦的声音就掉了下来。国王感到很奇怪。更羸说："那是一只受过伤的雁。它一听到我拉开弓弦的声响，就惊慌得支持不住，自然要掉下来了。"

"惊弓之鸟"这个成语比喻受过惊恐之后，有一点动静就特别害怕。

In the Warring States Period, there was a man in the State of Wei called Geng Lei. One day he said to the duke of the state, "I can shoot down birds by simply plucking my bowstring." When the duke expressed doubt about the truth of his claim, Geng Lei pointed his bow at a wild goose flying in the sky, twanged his bowstring, and the goose fell to the ground. Geng Lei said, "This goose has been injured in the past. Hearing the twang of the bowstring, it assumed that it was doomed. So it simply gave up trying to live."

This idiom means that if one has been frightened in the past, one may become paralysed when one faces a similar situation in the future.

Jīngwèi-tiánhǎi
23. 精卫填海

Jingwei fills up the sea

传说在远古时代，炎帝有一个女儿，一天她到东海去玩，不小心掉在海里淹死了。死后她变成了一只坚强、勇敢而美丽的小鸟，每天总是"精卫！精卫……"地叫，人们便叫她"精卫鸟"。她每天衔（xián）来西山上的木头或石头，投到东海里，决心要把东海填平。

"精卫填海"这个成语，比喻不怕艰难困苦，不达目的誓不罢休的坚强意志。

It is said that in ancient times King Yan had a daughter. One day she went to the Eastern Sea to play and accidentally drowned. After her death she became a brave and beautiful bird who cried every day. In imitation of her ceaseless cry, she was called the Jingwei bird. Every day she would pick up wood and pebbles from the Western Mountain and drop them into the Eastern Sea and was determined to fill it.

This idiom describes an indomitable will to achieve one's goal regardless of all difficulties.

Jǐngdǐ-zhīwā
24. 井底之蛙

A frog in a well

水井里居住着一只青蛙，它从来没有到外面去游玩过。一天，东海里来了一只鳖（biē）。青蛙非常得意地对它谈论起井底的"世界"是多么宽阔和美妙，并且邀（yāo）请鳖到井中来做客。鳖刚要进去，一只脚就被水井边的石头卡住了。于是，鳖把海洋如何宽广的情形讲给青蛙听。青蛙听了大吃一惊，感到非常惭愧。

"井底之蛙"这个成语用来讥笑人眼界狭小，见识短浅。

At the bottom of a well there lived a frog that had never left the well in its life. One day he was visited by a turtle from the Eastern Sea. The frog boasted to the turtle about the wideness and fineness of the well and invited him to be a guest in the well. When the turtle entered, one of his feet was trapped by stones beside the well. So instead of descending into the well, the turtle told the frog all about the broadness of the sea and the frog felt shocked and humbled.

This idiom is used to satirize those who are shallow or narrow-minded.

Kèzhōu-qiújiàn

25. 刻舟求剑

Notching the boat to find the sword

战国时期有个楚国人得到一把宝剑，非常珍爱。一天，他坐船过江，不小心把宝剑掉到江中去了。他急忙在剑掉下去的船舷（xián）边上刻了一个记号，说："我的剑是从这里掉下去的。"船靠岸后，他就从刻有记号的地方跳下水去找他的剑。船已经开走了，而剑并不能跟着船走，他怎么能找到宝剑呢？

"刻舟求剑"这个成语讽刺那些办事迂腐，不知道变通情况的人。

In the Warring States Period, a man in the State of Chu had a sword which he cherished very much. One day, while he was crossing a river in a boat, his sword suddenly fell into the water. The man then made a mark on the side of the boat at the spot where the sword had fallen overboard. When the boat reached the shore, he jumped from the spot he had marked on his boat into the water to look for his sword where it unsurprisingly couldn't be found.

This idiom satirizes those who stick to rigid rules without taking changed circumstances into account.

Kōngzhōng-lóugé

26. 空中楼阁

A castle in the air

一个有钱人要建筑师给他盖一座三层高的楼房。建筑师照着他的吩咐，挖土动工。第一层刚盖好，准备盖第二层的时候，这个有钱人却对建筑师说："我只要你盖第三层，而不要第一层和第二层！"建筑师说："没有第一层和第二层，怎么能修建第三层呢！"说完摇摇头拿上他的工具就走了。

"空中楼阁"这个成语比喻脱离实际、近乎幻想的理论或计划等。

A rich man asked an architect to build a three-story house for him. When the first story was finished, the rich man said to the architect, "I want only the third story; not the first and second stories." The architect asked, "Without the first and second stories, how can I build the third story?" Shaking his head, he packed up his tools and left.

This idiom describes unrealistic or impractical plans or theories.

Lànyú-chōngshù

27. 滥竽充数

Passing oneself off as a member of the orchestra

战国时代，齐宣王非常喜欢听吹竽，而且每次总要三百人同时吹。有一个南郭先生，本来不会吹竽，也混在中间凑数。后来，齐宣王死了，他的儿子齐湣（mǐn）王继位。湣王不喜欢听很多人同时吹竽，而要听一个人一个人地吹。南郭先生知道自己没有办法再混下去，就偷偷地溜走了。

"滥竽充数"这个成语比喻没有本领而冒充有本领，或者拿次货冒充好货。

In the Warring States Period, Duke Xuan of the State of Qi loved to listen to the *yu* — an ancient wind instrument. He would order 300 musicians at a time to play the yu for him. Mr. Nan Guo, who couldn't play the instrument, passed himself off as one of the musicians. When Duke Xuan died, his son Duke Min succeeded to the throne. Duke Min also loved the *yu*, but he preferred solo performances. Upon learning this, Mr. Nan Guo quietly slipped away from the orchestra.

This idiom is used to describe those who have no actual skills but pretend to be experts, or the passing off of inferior things as high-quality ones.

Lángbèi-wéijiān

28. 狼狈为奸

A wolf working hand in glove with a jackal

　　狼和狈常常结伴出外伤害牲畜。有一次，狼和狈一起来到一个羊圈外面。羊圈很高，又很坚固，叼不走里面的羊。狼和狈就想了一个办法：因为狼的前脚长后脚短，狈的前脚短后脚长，狼骑在狈的颈上，狈用长长的后脚站起来，狼就用长长的前脚攀（pān）住羊圈，终于把羊叼走。

　　"狼狈为奸"这个成语比喻坏人互相勾结起来干坏事。

A wolf and a jackal often went hunting together. Once they came to a sheepfold, the walls of which were firmly built and too high for them to get over. Then they had an idea: Since the wolf had long forelegs and short hindlegs while the jackal had short forelegs and long hindlegs, the wolf stood on the neck of the jackal, and the jackal stood up on its hindlegs. In this way the wolf could climb over the wall to get to where the sheep were.

This idiom is used to describe the act of doing evil things in collusion with others.

Lǎomǎ-shítú

29. 老马识途

An old horse knows the way

春秋时代，齐桓公出征攻打北方一个小国。去的时候是春天，遍地绿草茵茵。回来的时候是冬天，白雪茫茫，狂风怒吼，于是齐桓公的队伍迷失了方向。找不到回去的路，大家都很着急。这时，齐桓公的宰相管仲说："可以利用老马的经验。"于是齐桓公派人挑选了几匹老马在前面引路，果然走出了迷谷，找到了回去的道路。

"老马识途"这个成语用来比喻有经验的人，熟悉情况，办事效果好。

In the Spring and Autumn Period, Duke Huan of the State of Qi led an army to attack a small state in the north. They went there in spring when green grass covered the ground. However, when they came back it was winter. Everywhere was white with snow, the wind was howling all around and the troops lost their way. While everybody was worrying, Guan Zhong, the duke's prime minister, suggested, "Perhaps an old horse may know the way." So the duke ordered several old horses to be selected to lead the army and finally they found the way back home.

This idiom refers to the value of experience.

Liángshàng-jūnzǐ

30. 梁上君子

A gentleman on the beam

东汉（公元 25—220）时有个人叫陈寔（shí）。有一天晚上，一个小偷潜入他的房间，躲在房屋梁上，准备等主人睡熟以后下来偷东西。陈寔看见了，把子孙召集起来，大声对他们说："人应该有志气啊！坏人不是生来就坏，如果做坏事成了习惯，就难于改过来了。房梁上的那位君子就是这样的人！"小偷听见后，连忙跳下来磕（kē）头认罪。

人们借用这个故事，把偷东西的贼称为"梁上君子"。

In the Eastern Han Dynasty (25-220) there was a man called Chen Shi. One night, a thief slipped into his room. Hiding above the roof beam, the thief waited for Chen Shi to go to sleep. Chen Shi, noticing the thief, called his children and grandchildren together, saying, "To be a man one should have aspirations. Evildoers are not born evil. However, if one gets used to doing evil things, it will be hard for them to reform. The gentleman above the roof beam is such a man." The thief, hearing this, hurriedly jumped down and knelt on the ground before Chen Shi to beg his forgiveness.

This idiom is used to refer to a thief.

Línkě-juéjǐng

31. 临渴掘井

Not digging a well until one is thirsty

春秋时代，国君鲁昭公在鲁国待不下去，跑到了齐国。他对齐景公谈起自己过去的错误，感到很后悔。齐景公认为他应该回鲁国去，今后还可能成为一位贤明的国君。而齐国的官员晏子说："已经面临着威胁的人，才急着去铸（zhù）造兵器；吃东西噎（yē）住了咽喉的人，才急着去挖井取水。即使再快，也来不及了。"

"临渴掘井"这个成语比喻事前毫无准备，临到需要时，才急忙想办法。

In the Spring and Autumn Period, Duke Zhao of the State of Lu fled to the State of Qi, following palace turmoil. He admitted his mistakes to Duke Jing of Qi. Duke Jing advised him to go back to Lu, as he might become a wise ruler since he could recognize his faults. However Yanzi, an official of Qi, commented, "It is too late to make weapons when one is endangered, and too late to dig a well when one is choking on food and needs water desperately."

This idiom warns against being unprepared and having to seek solutions at the last moment.

Mǎnchéng-fēngyǔ

32. 满城风雨

A storm enveloping the city

北宋时期，有个很会写诗的人，叫潘大临。重阳节快要到了，风雨搅动着秋天的树林，潘大临诗兴大发，提笔写了一句很美的诗："满城风雨近重阳。"正要往下面写的时候，突然催税的人闯了进来，潘大临就再也没有诗兴往下面写了。

以后人们用"满城风雨"这个成语形容某个消息或事情一经传出，到处议论纷纷。

In the Northern Song Dynasty (960-1127), there was a man called Pan Dalin who was a renowned poet. As the Double Ninth Festival approached, the trees swayed in the autumn wind and rain. The poet, inspired by the scene wrote a beautiful line, "The Double Ninth Festival is approaching with wind and rain sweeping across the town." Just as he wrote this, the local tax collector came to demand payment from him, instantly vanishing all Pan's inspiration.

Later, the first part of the line came to be used as a set phrase meaning "the talk of the town".

Mángrén-mōxiàng

33. 盲人摸象

Blind men touching an elephant

有几个盲人在一起，想知道象究竟是什么东西。有一个摸着象的门牙说"象像一根大萝卜"；有一个摸着象的耳朵说"象像一把大扇子"；有一个摸着象的腿说"象像一根大柱子"；有一个摸着象的身躯说"象像一堵墙"；有一个摸着象的尾巴说"象像一条蛇"。他们争论不休，都认为自己说得不错。

"盲人摸象"这个故事用来比喻那些片面观察事物的人，不了解事物的整体或本质。

A group of blind men gathered around an elephant, trying to find out what the creature looked like. One of them happened to touch one of the tusks and said, "An elephant is just like a turnip." Another touched one of the elephant's ears and said, "It is like a big fan." One put his arms around one of the beast's legs, and said, "It is like a column." One who happened to place his hands on the body of the elephant said, "It is like a wall." The one who got hold of the tail said, "It is like a snake." They then fell to arguing with each other.

This idiom is used to satirize those who only know part of a thing but not its entirety or essence.

Máosuì-zìjiàn

34. 毛遂自荐

Mao Sui recommending himself

战国时代，秦国军队攻打赵国的都城。赵国的平原君打算亲自到楚国去请救兵，想挑选一个精明能干的人一同前去。有一个名叫毛遂的人，自告奋勇原意同去。平原君到楚国后，与楚王谈了半天，没有一点结果。毛遂怒气冲冲地拿着宝剑，逼近楚王，终于迫使楚王答应出兵，与赵国联合共同抵抗秦国。

"毛遂自荐"这个成语用来比喻自己推荐自己，不必别人介绍。

In the Warring States Period, the State of Qin besieged the capital of the State of Zhao. Duke Pingyuan of Zhao planned to ask the ruler of the State of Chu personally for assistance. He wanted to select a capable man to go with him. A man called Mao Sui volunteered. When the negotiations between the two states were stalled because the ruler of Chu hesitated to send troops, Mao Sui approached him while angrily brandishing a sword. At that, the ruler of Chu agreed to help Zhao fight against Qin.

This idiom means to recommend oneself.

Méntíng-ruòshì

35. 门庭若市

A courtyard as crowded as a marketplace

战国时代，齐威王接受了大臣邹忌（jì）的建议，决心广泛听取意见，治理国家。于是他发布了一条命令："不管是朝廷的臣子或地方的官吏和百姓，凡能够当面指责我的过失的受上赏；上书规劝我的受中赏；在公共场所议论和批评我的过失、让我知道的受下赏。"命令公布以后，大家纷纷跑到齐威王那里去提意见，王宫的大门口和庭院里热闹得像市场一样。

后来，"门庭若市"变成一个成语，用来形容来往人多，非常热闹的景象。

In the Warring States Period, Duke Wei of the State of Qi accepted the suggestion of his minister Zou Ji to gather opinions on ruling the state from far and wide. He issued a notice, saying "Regardless of whether a man is a minister or a commoner, anyone who can point out my faults to my face will win first prize; anyone who advises me in a memorial will win second prize; anyone who criticizes me publicly will win third prize." When they learnt about this, the people flocked to the duke's palace to present their opinions. The area in front of the palace gate was as busy as a marketplace.

From this story is derived the idiom which describes a very busy scene filled with people.

Míngluò-sūnshān

36. 名落孙山

Failing to pass an examination

宋朝（公元 960—1279）时有一个擅（shàn）长幽默（yōumò）的人，名叫孙山。有一年，他去参加科举考试。榜发出来，孙山考上了最后一名。回到家乡，一位同乡向他打听自己的儿子考上没有。孙山笑了一笑说："孙山考上最后一名，您儿子的名字还在孙山后面呢。"

后来人们用"名落孙山"来比喻考试没有考上或者选拔没有被录取。

In the Song Dynasty (960-1279) there was a man with a good sense of humour called Sun Shan. One year he went to take the imperial examination and came last on the list of successful candidates. Back in his hometown, one of his neighbours asked him whether that neighbour's son had also passed. Sun Shan said with a smile, "Sun Shan was the last on the list. Your son came after Sun Shan."

Later, people used this idiom to indicate failing in an examination or competition.

Nányuán-běizhé

37. 南辕^① 北辙^②

Going south by driving the chariot north

---

① 辕：车前驾牲口的木头。(shafts of a cart)

② 辙：车轮压出的痕迹，指道路。(the track of a wheel, referring to a road)

从前有个人要到南方去，他坐的车子却向北方行驶。过路人说："你去南方，车子怎么向北行驶呢？"他回答说："我的马很能跑路，我的车夫驾车的技术也很高明，加上我又带了充足的路费。"这个人没有考虑到，方向弄反了，他的条件越好，离他要去的地方就越远。

后来人们就把这个故事概括为"南辕北辙"，比喻一个人的行动和他的目的正好相反。

Once a man wanted to go to the south, but his chariot was heading north. A passer-by asked him, "If you are going to the south, why is your chariot heading north?" The man answered, "My horse is good at running, my driver is highly skilled at driving a carriage, and I have enough money with me." The man didn't consider that the direction might be wrong or that the better his conditions were, the further he was away from his destination.

The idiom derived from this story describes when one's action has the opposite effect upon one's intention.

Nùfà-chōngguān
38. 怒发冲冠

So angry that one's hair lifts up one's hat

战国时代，赵国的大臣蔺相如出使到秦国。在他向秦王索回玉璧（bì）的时候，秦王蛮（mán）不讲理，蔺相如气愤得连头发都竖了起来，向上冲着帽子。

后来人们用"怒发冲冠"这个成语形容人愤怒到了极点。

In the Warring States Period, Lin Xiangru, minister of the State of Zhao, was sent as an envoy to the State of Qin to ask the ruler of Qin to return a fine piece of jade to Zhao. However, the ruler of Qin was rude and unreasonable. Lin became so angry with him, his hair stood up so stiffly on his head that it lifted up his hat.

This idiom came to be used to mean being extremely angry.

Pījǐng-zhǎnjí

39. 披荆斩棘

Clearing a way through thistles and thorns

东汉的第一个皇帝叫刘秀。在刘秀打天下的时候，冯异立过很多战功，得到刘秀的信任。后来有人借故诬告冯异，刘秀当着大臣的面说："冯异是我打天下的助手，替我劈开了前进道路上的荆棘 [①]（比喻扫除了障碍），我才获得了成功。"

后来人们根据上面的故事，造出"披荆斩棘"这个成语，用来比喻扫除前进道路上的种种障碍，奋勇前进。

The first emperor of the Eastern Han Dynasty, Liu Xiu, greatly trusted a man named Feng Yi who had helped him attain the throne. When someone slandered Feng Yi, Liu Xiu told his ministers, "Feng Yi helped me to gain power. I succeeded because he broke through all the thistles and thorns in my way (removed all obstacles in my path)."

The idiom derived from this story means to clear away difficulties and bravely advance.

---

① 荆棘：丛生的多刺植物。(thistle and thorn)

Pífú-hànshù

40. 蚍蜉撼树

An ant trying to shake a big tree

韩愈是唐朝（公元 618—907）时候著名的文学家。他在一首诗里写过这样的两句话："蚍蜉撼大树，可笑不自量。"蚍蜉是一种大蚂蚁，它自认为力量很大，可以把大树摇动，真是太可笑了。

"蚍蜉撼树"这个成语以后用来比喻力量很小却妄想动摇强大的事物。

Han Yu was a famous poet of the Tang Dynasty (618-907). In one of his poems he wrote, "An ant tries to topple a giant tree, ridiculously overrating its ability."

This idiom later was used to refer to overestimating one's power and trying to overthrow someone or something much stronger and more powerful than oneself.

Pòfǔ-chénzhōu

41. 破釜 ① 沉舟

Smashing the cauldrons and sinking the boats

---

① 釜：古代的锅。(an ancient pot)

秦朝（公元前221—公元前206）末年，楚霸王项羽率领部队与秦军作战。部队渡过漳河以后，项羽命令士兵把所有的船只都毁掉沉到河底，把行军的饭锅全部打碎，每人只发给三天的粮食。项羽这样做的目的，是向大家表示只能胜利前进、不能失败后退的决心。果然，部队经过九次激烈的战斗，终于打垮了秦军。

"破釜沉舟"这个成语比喻下定最后的决心，不顾一切干到底。

During the late years of the Qin Dynasty (221-206 BC), Xiang Yu led a rebellion. After crossing the Zhang River, Xiang Yu ordered his men to sink all their boats and break their cauldrons. He issued each soldier three days' rations and warned them that there was no way to retreat; the only thing they could do to survive was to advance and fight. After nine fierce battles, the Qin army was finally defeated.

This idiom is used to indicate one's firm determination to achieve one's goal at any cost.

Pòjìng-chóngyuán

42. 破镜重圆

A broken mirror made whole again

　　南朝陈国（公元 557—589）将要灭亡的时候，驸马徐德言把一面铜镜破开，跟妻子各留下一半。双方约定：如果将来夫妻失散了，就把它当做信物。后来，夫妻二人真的失散了。凭借着各人留下的半面镜子，他们最终又得以团圆。

　　"破镜重圆"这个成语比喻夫妻失散或分离后重新团聚。

In the Southern Dynasties when the State of Chen (557-589) was facing its demise, Xu Deyan, husband of the princess, broke a bronze mirror in two. Each of them kept a half as a token in case they were separated. Soon afterwards, they did lose touch with each other, but the two halves of the mirror helped them to be reunited.

This idiom is used to refer to the reunion of a couple after they lose touch or break up.

Qíhǔ-nánxià

43. 骑虎难下

When one rides a tiger it is hard to dismount

北周最后一个皇帝年龄很小，大臣杨坚掌握了国家大权。杨坚的妻子劝告杨坚说："北周已经不行了。你现在就像骑在老虎背上，形势逼迫着你不能下来，只好干下去吧！"杨坚觉得很有道理，后来就自己当了皇帝，建立了隋朝（公元581—618），并且统一了中国。

"骑虎难下"这个成语用来比喻做事中途遇到很大困难，但形势所迫，又不能中止。

Yang Jian acted as the regent of the last emperor of Northern Zhou (557-581) as the emperor was very young. His wife advised him, "Northern Zhou is dying. Now, it is as if you are riding on the back of a tiger — it will be dangerous to dismount. You can do nothing but continue." Yang thought this piece of advice quite rational. Later, he founded the Sui Dynasty (581-618), and united China once more.

This idiom is used as a metaphor meaning that when one is in a difficult situation, one cannot do anything but continue to pursue one's course.

Qǐrén-yōutiān

44. 杞人忧天

The man of Qi who worried that the sky would fall

春秋时代，杞国有一个喜欢胡思乱想的人。一天，他竟然想到，天会塌下来，地会陷下去，自己到哪里去安身？这个人越想越害怕，整天愁眉苦脸，坐立不安，白天吃不下饭，晚上睡不着觉。后来有人耐心地开导他，他才放下了心。

"杞人忧天"这个成语讥笑那些没有必要或毫无根据的忧虑。

In the Spring and Autumn Period, there was a man in the State of Qi who always let his imagination run away with him. One day he worried that the sky would fall on his head, the ground would sink, and he would have no place to live. He became so worried that he was on tenterhooks every day and could neither eat nor sleep. Later, someone patiently persuaded him that his fears were groundless and he finally relaxed.

This idiom satirizes those who worry unnecessarily or groundlessly.

Qiánlǘ-jìqióng

45. 黔^①驴技穷

The Guizhou donkey has exhausted its tricks

---

① 黔：贵州省的别称。(another name for Guizhou Province)

从前，贵州没有驴子。有人从外地带回一头驴子，拴在山下。一只老虎看到了，以为是什么怪物，急忙躲到树林中去偷偷地瞧。驴子大叫一声，老虎吓了一跳，以为驴子要吃掉自己。时间一长，老虎觉得驴子并没有什么恶意，逐渐走近去戏弄它，触犯它。驴子生气了，用蹄子踢老虎。老虎心里想："你的本领不过就是如此啊！"于是立即扑过去，一口把它咬死吃掉了。

"黔驴技穷"这个成语比喻仅有的一点本事也用完了，再没有别的办法了。

In ancient times there were no donkeys in Guizhou Province. However, somebody brought a donkey from somewhere and tied it to a tree at the foot of a mountain. A tiger saw the donkey and thought that it must be a fearsome monster. It hid behind a tree and spied on the donkey. When the donkey brayed, the tiger was frightened, thinking that the donkey was about to devour it. However, after a while, seeing that the donkey had not moved, the tiger approached it and began to tease it. This made the donkey angry, so it kicked the tiger. The tiger thought to itself, "Is that all it is capable of?" It then pounced on the donkey and ate it.

This idiom is used to mean that one has exhausted one's skills or options.

Rìmù-túqióng

46. 日暮① 途穷②

The day is waning and the road is ending

---

① 日暮：天色晚了。(late in the day)

② 途穷：路到头了。(to come to the end of a road)

春秋时代，楚平王听信谗（chán）言，杀了伍子胥（xū）的父亲。伍子胥逃到吴国，十多年后帮助吴王打到楚国的都城，报了仇。伍子胥虽然报了仇，但是受到国人的责备。伍子胥内心十分痛苦，说："我就像一个行路的人，天已经晚了，而路途还十分遥远，不知该怎么办啊！"

这个故事后来变成成语"日暮途穷"，比喻处境十分困难，力量用尽了，计策没有了。

In the Spring and Autumn Period, Duke Ping of Chu was misled by slanderers, and had Wu Zixu's father executed. Wu Zixu then fled to the State of Wu. More than ten years later, Wu Zixu took his revenge by helping Wu conquer Chu. Yet he suffered agonies of remorse because his countrymen called him a traitor. He protested, "I'm like a traveller. It's late, but I still have a long way to go. I simply don't know what to do."

This idiom comes from the above story. It means being in a very difficult situation or at the end of one's tether and resources.

Rúhuǒ-rútú

47. 如火如荼 ①

Like a raging fire

---

① 荼：开白花的茅草。(a kind of reed with white tufts)

春秋时代，吴王夫差想做几个小国的霸主，率领三万军队向晋军挑战。他命令将士们以一万人为单位摆成一个正方形的阵势。当中的都穿白色衣服，拿着白色的旗帜，远远望去就像遍地盛开着白色茶花。左边的穿红色衣服，拿着红色的旗帜，远远望去就像满山燃烧着熊熊火焰。右边的穿黑色衣服，拿着黑色的旗帜，远远望去像是满天结集着浓密的乌云。夫差想利用这种声势去压倒对方。

"如火如荼"这个成语形容气势旺盛、场面热烈的景象。

During the Spring and Autumn Period, Duke Fuchai of Wu led a huge army against the State of Jin. He ordered his men to form three square contingents. The middle one was dressed in white and holding white flags, which looked from a distance just like the flowers of a field full of reeds. The left unit was in red and holding red flags, which looked from afar like flaming fire all over the mountains. The right unit was in black and holding black flags, which looked from a distance like thick black clouds covering the sky. Fuchai was trying to present to the enemy a show of overwhelming force.

This idiom describes a scene of great majesty and power.

Rúyú-déshuǐ

48. 如鱼得水

To feel just like a fish in water

三国时代，刘备为了夺得天下，曾经三次到湖北隆中请诸葛（gě）亮出来，辅佐自己。诸葛亮出来以后，协助刘备处理军政大事，得到刘备的高度信任，两人感情越来越好。刘备对手下人说："我有了孔明（诸葛亮的'字'），就好像鱼儿有了水一样。"

"如鱼得水"这个成语比喻得到了和自己非常投合的人，或所处环境对自己非常适合。

In the Three Kingdoms Period, Liu Bei, the founding emperor of the State of Shu Han, went to Longzhong in Hubei Province three times to ask Zhuge Liang, an accomplished strategist, to assist him. Finally, Zhuge Liang agreed to help Liu Bei deal with military affairs and politics, and became greatly trusted by the latter. Over time, their regard for each other became deeper and deeper. Liu Bei described their friendship to his ministers thus, "Having Kongming (the style name of Zhuge Liang) assist me, I feel just like a stranded fish which has been put back in the water."

This idiom is used to describe finding a boon companion or an ideal situation.

Rùmù-sānfēn

49. 入木三分

To enter three-tenths of an inch into the timber

东晋时代的王羲（xī）之，是中国杰出的书法家。他的字写得既秀丽，又苍劲有力。他平时勤学苦练，即使休息时间也在揣摩（chuǎimó）字体的结构，手不停地在衣服上画。时间长了，衣服都画破了。传说有一次他在木板上写字，刻字的人惊奇地发现，他所写的字，墨汁透入木板竟有三分深！

"入木三分"原本形容王羲之的书法很有功力。后来比喻分析问题十分深刻。

Wang Xizhi was a prominent calligrapher of the Eastern Jin Dynasty (317-420). His style was beautiful, bold and vigorous. He was very diligent about practising; even when resting, he would engage in figuring out the structure of characters by "writing" on his clothes. With the passage of time, his clothes were worn out by rubbing. It is said that once a carpenter found that the ink of the characters Wang Xizhi had written on a plank had soaked almost one centimetre into it.

This idiom originally described the vigour of Wang Xizhi's handwriting. Later, it came to be used to mean penetrating analysis.

Sàiwēng-shīmǎ

50. 塞翁失马

The old man who lost his horse

古时候，边塞上有个老人丢了一匹马。邻居知道了，怕他过于悲伤，特地前来安慰他。老人却说："丢了马本来是一件坏事，但是怎么能知道它不会变成一件好事呢？"过了几个月，丢失的那匹马竟然带着一匹骏马跑了回来。

"塞翁失马"这个成语比喻暂时的损失或挫折，也许因此会得到好处。或者说，坏事在一定条件下可以变成好事。

In ancient times, an old man living on the frontier lost a horse. His neighbour came to comfort him, but the old man just said, "Losing a horse might be a bad thing, but it might turn out to be a good thing as well. Who can tell?" A few months later, the lost horse came back, bringing with it another fine steed.

This idiom is used metaphorically to mean that sometimes people may benfit from a temporary loss or setback. In other words, a calamity may turn into a blessing.

Sāngù-máolú

51. 三顾 ^① 茅庐 ^②

Paying three visits to the cottage

---

① 顾：拜访。(to visit)

② 茅庐：草屋。(thatched cottage)

三国时，诸葛亮居住在隆中的茅庐里，刘备听说诸葛亮很有学识，又有才能，就带着礼物去请他出来辅佐自己打天下。刘备一共去了三次，最后才见到诸葛亮。诸葛亮见刘备十分诚恳，终于答应了他的请求。从此，诸葛亮用全部精力辅佐刘备，在军事上和政治上取得了巨大的胜利。

"三顾茅庐"这个成语用来比喻诚心诚意地一再邀请人家。

In the Three Kingdoms Period, Zhuge Liang lived in seclusion in a thatched cottage. Liu Bei, hearing that Zhuge Liang was very knowledgeable and capable, went to visit him with gifts, hoping that Zhuge Liang would agree to assist him with state affairs. He had to make three visits before Zhuge Liang agreed to do so because he was impressed by Liu Bei's sincerity. From then on, Zhuge Liang helped Liu Bei whole-heartedly and made great achievements in both the military and political spheres.

This idiom means to persist in inviting someone with sincerity.

Sānrén-chénghǔ

52. 三人成虎

Repeat a lie enough times and it will be believed

战国时代，魏王的臣子庞（páng）葱问魏王：
"现在有一个人说街上有老虎，你相信吗？"魏
王说："不相信。"庞葱又问："两个人说街上有老
虎，你相信吗？"魏王表示有点怀疑。庞葱又问：
"三个人说街上有老虎，你相信吗？"魏王说："我
相信了。"庞葱说："街上没有老虎是很明显的事，
然而三个人都说有老虎你就相信了。要警惕谣言
变成真话呀！"

"三人成虎"比喻谣言多次流传，就可能使
人信以为真。

In the Warring States Period, Pang Cong, a minister of
the State of Wei, said to the Duke of Wei, "Someone said that
there are tigers in the streets. Do you believe this?" The duke
answered, "No, I don't believe it." Pang Cong said later, "Now
two people have said that there are tigers in the streets. Do
you believe now?" The duke showed some doubt. Then Pang
Cong said, "Now three people have said the same thing. Do
you believe it now?" The duke said, "Yes, I do." Pang Cong
continued, "There are no tigers in the streets at all. Yet if three
people say the same thing, you believe it! We must be alert to
the danger of rumours gaining credence."

This idiom refers to the fact that a rumour, if repeated
often enough, may come to be believed.

Sàng jiā-zhīquǎn

53. 丧家之犬

A homeless dog

春秋时代，孔子带着弟子们周游列国，到处游说，可是四处碰壁。一次走到郑国，孔子与弟子们走散了。孔子站在东城门外，一个人孤零零的。有一个郑国人看到后，讥笑孔子说："看他那副样子，真像一条丧家之犬！"孔子听见后笑了笑，不在意地说："是啊，是啊，真是有点像啊！"

"丧家之犬"本意是指办丧事人家的狗，后来转指无家可归的狗。比喻失去依靠、无处投奔的人。

In the Spring and Autumn Period, Confucius took his disciples on visits to various states. They offered their services everywhere, but were always rebuffed. One day, in the State of Zheng, Confucius lost his disciples. He stood outside the east gate by himself. A citizen of Zheng then mocked Confucius, "Look at him," he said. "Isn't he like a stray cur?" Hearing this, Confucius smiled and said calmly, "Yes, yes indeed."

This idiom originally referred to dogs of families in mourning. Later it came to describe homeless dogs, and metaphorically refer to people with nowhere to go and no one to turn to.

Shā jǐ-xiàhóu

54. 杀鸡吓猴

Killing the chicken to frighten the monkeys

古时候，有一个人养了许多猴子。猴子长大后，变得越来越调皮，常常不听主人的话，还弄坏主人的东西，主人很生气。一天，主人捉来一只公鸡，把猴子们叫到跟前，对它们说："你们若是再捣乱，不听话，就像这只鸡一样。"说着，就当着猴子们的面把公鸡杀了。猴子们见到血淋淋的公鸡，非常害怕，以后就变得老实多了。

"杀鸡吓猴"比喻惩罚一个人来吓唬另外一个人或一些人。

In ancient times, there was a man who raised a lot of monkeys. These monkeys became more and more mischievous as they grew up and often destroyed his things, so the man became very angry with them. One day the man caught a rooster, assembled the monkeys and said to them, "If you don't behave and stop causing trouble, you will end up like this rooster." Then he killed the rooster right in front of them. Seeing this, the monkeys were frightened and became obedient thereafter.

This idiom is used metaphorically to mean to frighten or to warn somebody by punishing someone else.

Shènxiāo-chénshàng
55. 甚①囂②尘上

Making a great clamour

---

① 甚: 很，极。(extremely)

② 囂: 喧闹。(noise, bustle)

战国时代，晋国和楚国交战。楚共王站在架有高台的战车上观察晋军的动静。看了一会儿，楚共王说："那边人声十分喧嚣，而且尘土都飞扬起来了！"部下说："这是他们在填井平灶，摆开阵势要作战啦！"

"甚嚣尘上"这个成语，现在比喻对传闻的事情议论纷纷。

Once in the Warring States Period, the State of Jin was at war with the State of Chu. Duke Gong of Chu stood on a high platform built on a chariot and watched the movements of the Jin army. After watching for a while, he said, "It's quite noisy over there and cloud of dust has been kicked up." His aide answered, "The enemy are filling up the wells and destroying their cooking stoves. They are preparing to fight."

This idiom is now used to mean a lot of commotion over hearsay.

Shìrú-pòzhú

56. 势如破竹

Like splitting bamboo

晋朝时候，大将军杜预带兵攻打吴国，一路上打了很多胜仗。有人认为应该暂时休整一下，第二年再继续进攻。杜预说："现在我们的士气正旺盛，攻打吴国就像劈竹子一样，等到劈开几节之后，下面的就会迎刃而解了。"后来杜预果然灭掉了吴国。

"势如破竹"这个成语比喻作战或工作节节胜利，势不可挡。另一个成语"迎刃而解"比喻主要问题解决了，其他有关问题就可以顺利地解决。

In the Jin Dynasty, General Du Yu led troops to attack the State of Wu. He achieved victory after victory along the route. Somebody suggested that they should stop and rest until the following year, but Du Yu said, "At the moment the morale of our troops is very high. Attacking Wu will be just like splitting bamboo. After splitting open the first few joints, the rest will be easily broken apart." So he went on to eliminate the State of Wu.

This idiom means to win a victory with irresistible force. Another idiom, 迎刃而解, means that if a major problem is solved, other relevant problems will be settled easily.

Shìwài-táoyuán

57. 世外桃源

A haven of peace and happiness

东晋的文学家陶渊明写了一篇著名的文章叫
《桃花源记》。文章叙述一个渔人出外捕鱼的时候，
偶然来到了桃花源这个地方。从这里通过一个山
洞，发现了一个村子，这里的居民是秦朝时避难
人的后代。这是一个与世隔绝、没有剥削和压迫、
人人安居乐业的美好社会。渔人告别村民回家以
后，再也找不到这个地方了。

后来，由这个故事产生了"世外桃源"这个
成语，用来比喻与世隔绝的、理想的美好世界。

Tao Yuanming, a famous writer of the Eastern Jin
Dynasty, wrote the well-known essay *Peach-Blossom Spring*.
In it he tells a story which goes like this: A fisherman happened to come upon a place called Peach-Blossom Spring.
Squeezing through a cave, he found a village, the residents of
which were descendants of refugees from the Qin Dynasty.
It was a paradise isolated from the outside world, without
exploitation or oppression, where everybody lived and
worked in peace and contentment. The fisherman left the
villagers and went home. However, no mather how hard he
searched, he could never again find the place.

This idiom is derived from the above story, and is used
to mean an isolated, ideal world.

Shǒubú-shìjuàn

58. 手不释① 卷②

Always with a book in hand

---

① 释：放下。(to put down)
② 卷：书籍。(book)

吕蒙是三国时代吴国的一员大将，曾经立过不少战功。吕蒙小时候家境贫苦，没能上学读书。他当了大将以后，国王孙权鼓励他要多读书。吕蒙听从了孙权的建议，每天坚持不懈、专心致志地读书，哪怕是在行军作战的紧张时刻，他也挤出时间来学习，手里总是不丢开书本。后来吕蒙终于成为一名学识渊博的将军。

"手不释卷"这个成语形容人学习十分用功。

Lü Meng was a meritorious general of the State of Wu during the Three Kingdoms Period. He came from a poor family and had not had the chance to go to school when he was young. When he became a general, the Emperor of Wu encouraged him to read books. Lü Meng took his advice, and started to read persistently and devotedly. Even when he was marching or fighting, he would still find time to study. There was always a book in his hand. Finally, Lü Meng became a learned general.

This idiom is used to describe being diligent in one's studies.

Shǒuzhū-dàitù

59. 守株^① 待兔

Sitting by a stump, waiting for a careless hare

---

① 株：树桩。(tree stump)

春秋时代，宋国有个农夫在耕田的时候，忽然跑来一只兔子恰巧碰到树桩上，脖子折断死了。农夫把兔子拾回家去，美美地吃了一顿兔肉。晚上他想："我何必辛辛苦苦地种地呢？每天在树下能捡到一只兔子就够我吃的了。"于是，他从此不再耕作，每天坐在树下等待兔子的到来。

"守株待兔"这个成语，讥笑那些存在侥幸心理，不想经过努力就希望得到意外收获的人。

In the Spring and Autumn Period, a farmer in the State of Song was working one day in the fields when he saw a hare bump into a tree stump accidentally, break its neck and die. The farmer took the hare home and cooked himself a delicious meal. That night he thought, "I needn't work so hard. All I have to do is wait for a hare each day by the stump." So from then on he gave up farming, and simply sat by the stump waiting for hares to come and run into it.

This idiom satirizes those who just wait for a stroke of luck, rather than making efforts to obtain what they need.

Shǔquǎn-fèirì

60. 蜀^① 犬吠^② 日

A Sichuan dog barks at the sun

---

① 蜀：四川省的别称。(another name for Sichuan Province)

② 吠：狗叫。(to bark)

唐朝（公元 618—907）著名的文学家柳宗元，曾经讲过一个"蜀犬吠日"的故事。在中国西南地区的四川省，那里的气候多雨多雾，有时阴雨连绵、雾气蒙蒙长达数月，一年四季很难看见太阳。所以那里的狗一见到太阳出来，都感到很新奇，就大声狂叫起来。

"蜀犬吠日"这个成语比喻少见多怪（对本来是很平常的事情，由于见识短浅而感到奇怪）。

A leading writer of the Tang Dynasty, Liu Zongyuan, related how, in Sichuan Province in southwest China, it was cloudy and foggy most of the year and that the sun was hardly ever seen. So when the sun came out, the local dogs would feel that something strange was happening and bark loudly.

This idiom is used to mean being surprised at something normal due to one's ignorance.

Shùzhī-gāogé

61. 束 ^① 之高阁

Putting it on a high shelf

---

① 束：捆。(to tie up)

晋朝（公元 265—420）时候有个叫殷（yīn）浩的人，很有才能，又善于辩论，后来当了将军。可是在一次战争中他打了败仗，被免了官，在家闲着。有人建议请殷浩再次出来做官。另一个叫做庾（yǔ）翼的将军听见了，不同意这个建议。他对人说："像殷浩这样的人，只应该把他捆起来放到高高的架子上，等天下太平了，再请他出来做官吧。"

后来人们就用"束之高阁"这个成语比喻把某人、某种东西或某件事物扔在一边，不去利用它。

In the Jin Dynasty, there was a man called Yin Hao who was both capable and eloquent. However, failure in a battle caused him to lose his position as a general. Someone once suggested assigning Yin Hao to be a general again, but a general called Yu Yi did not agree, saying, "All we can do with someone like Yin Hao is tie him up and put him on a high shelf. We should not assign him to a position again until the country is at peace."

Later this idiom was used to mean putting aside and ignoring something or someone.

Shuǐluò-shíchū

62. 水落石出

When the water ebbs, stones will appear

北宋时代的大文学家苏东坡，贬（biǎn）官到了湖北黄州。他两次到黄州赤壁游览，写下了著名的《前赤壁赋》和《后赤壁赋》。在后面一篇文章中，有"山高月小，水落石出"的著名句子。其中"水落石出"描述了长江的景象：江水下落，原来被淹没在水下面的石头有的就显露出来了。

"水落石出"这个成语用来比喻经过反复调查以后，事实的真相终于彻底弄明白了。

In the Northern Song Dynasty, the poet Su Dongpo was once banished to Huangzhou in Hubei Province. There he visited the Red Cliff twice and wrote prose pieces called "The First Visit to the Red Cliff" and "The Second Visit to the Red Cliff". In the latter work, there is a line which goes, "High mountains and small moon, the rocks emerge when the water subsides."

This idiom is used metaphorically to mean that the truth comes to light after repeated investigation.

Sìmiàn-chǔgē

63. 四面楚歌

Songs of Chu on all sides

　　秦朝末年，楚和汉争夺天下。楚王项羽被汉王刘邦的军队紧紧地围困在垓（gāi）下这个地方。项羽的兵士已经很少，粮食也没有了，危急万分。夜里，四面包围着的汉军唱起了楚地的民歌。项羽听了，非常吃惊地说："汉军已经全部占领了楚国的土地吗？为什么在汉军中有这么多的人会唱楚歌呢？"说着就从床上爬起来，带着残余的士兵惊慌地逃走了。

　　"四面楚歌"这个成语比喻四面受到敌人的攻击，处于孤立危急的困境。

At the end of the Qin Dynasty, the State of Chu and the State of Han fought for control of the country. Xiang Yu, the King of Chu, was besieged at a place called Gaixia by the Han army led by Liu Bang. Xiang Yu was in a desperate situation, with little food and only a few soldiers. At night, the surrounding Han troops started to sing Chu folk songs. Xiang Yu was very surprised at this, and said, "Has Liu Bang occupied the whole of Chu? Why are there so many Han soldiers who can sing Chu folk songs?" Then he fled with the remainder of his forces.

This idiom means to be in a helpless and critical situation, surrounded by the enemy on all sides.

Tánhǔ-sèbiàn

64. 谈虎色变

Turn pale at the mention of a tiger

从前有一个人给大家讲老虎伤人的故事，讲得有声有色，周围的人都听得津津有味。其中一个农夫有一次在山上砍柴时曾被一只老虎咬伤，差点送了命。所以这个农夫听了老虎的故事，尤其感到害怕，脸的颜色都改变了。

"谈虎色变"这个成语比喻一提到可怕的事情，就表现出非常紧张、恐怖的样子。

Once upon a time, a man was telling stories about how tigers can injure people. Among the listeners there was a farmer who had once been attacked by a tiger and almost lost his life. After hearing this story, he became so frightened that his face turned pale.

This idiom means to look nervous and fearful when something awful is mentioned.

Tánhuā-yíxiàn

65. 昙花一现

A flower that vanishes as soon as it blooms

　　昙花是一种美丽而珍贵的花。这种花多在夜间开放，开花的时间又极短，很快就凋谢了，所以人们难得看见。按照佛教的传说，金轮王出世，昙花才能生长出来，极力形容昙花难得出现。

　　"昙花一现"比喻事物或人物出现不久就消失了。

The broad-leafed epiphyllum is a beautiful and precious flower which usually blooms at night, with its blossom only lasting for a brief period. According to a Buddhist legend, the plant blooms only upon the appearance of a divine king, which is a great rarity.

This idiom describes things which disappear shortly after they come into being.

Tángbì-dāngchē

66. 螳臂当^①车

A mantis trying to halt a cart

---

① 当：阻挡。(to obstruct)

这是一则寓言。

从前有一个车夫驾着马车在路上行驶。忽然前面跳来一只螳螂，举起镰刀一样的前腿，恶狠狠地挡住车轮前进。车夫没有理会它，车轮就从螳螂的身上压了过去。

"螳臂当车"这个成语比喻不估计自己的力量，去做办不到的事情，必然要遭到失败。也说"螳臂挡车"。

Fable has it that, once, a cart driver was driving his cart when a mantis jumped out in front of him. Raising its forelegs, it tried to obstruct the passage of the cart. Of course, it was crushed by one of the wheels.

This idiom is used to mean overrating oneself and trying to do what is beyond one's ability. The result can be nothing but failure. It also appears as 螳臂挡车.

Tiānhuā-luànzhuì

67. 天花乱坠

As if it were raining flowers

南北朝梁武帝的时候，有一个名叫云光的法师，讲经讲得很好。传说他有一次登坛（tán）讲经，感动了天上的花神。花神把天上的花纷纷降落下来，洒遍了大地。

"天花乱坠"这个成语后来比喻说话有声有色，非常动听（多指夸大的或不切实际的讲话）。

In the Southern and Northern Dynasties, during the reign of Emperor Wu of Liang, there was a monk called Master Yun Guang who was a very accomplished preacher. Once he explained the sutra so profoundly and subtly that the God of Flowers was moved and sent divine flowers down to Earth. Soon, the land was covered with flowers.

This idiom was later used to describe talking in a vivid and eloquent way (mostly in an exaggerated and impractical manner).

Tiānyá-hǎijiǎo

68. 天涯海角

The end of the sky and the corner of the sea

天的边缘（天涯），海的角落（海角），都是指非常遥远的地方。位于中国最南端的海南岛，自古以来被人们认为是"天涯海角"。北宋时代的大文学家苏轼，晚年被贬官来到这个地方。传说海南岛最南面巨石上的"天涯"两个字，就是苏轼写的。

这个成语用来形容极远的地方。或者两个人彼此相隔遥远。

"The edge of sky and the corner of the sea" both refer to the remotest places in existence. Hainan Island, located in the southernmost part of China, was considered the remotest place in ancient times. Su Shi, a famous poet of the Northern Song Dynasty, was exiled there in his later years. It is said that the two characters 天涯 on a huge rock on the southernmost tip of the island were written by Su Shi.

This idiom refers to the remotest places or a very long distance between two people.

Tiānyī-wúfèng

69. 天衣无缝

Divine garments without seams

唐朝有个人叫郭翰（hàn）。一个夏天的晚上，月光非常明亮。他忽然看见天空中有个女子轻盈而缓慢地飘落下来。他仔细地观察那个女子，发现她身上穿的衣服连一条缝（fèng）也没有，感到非常奇怪，便问那个女子。女子回答说："天衣本来就用不着针线缝（féng）合的呀！"

"天衣无缝"这个成语用来比喻处理事情十分周密，不露一点痕迹。也比喻诗文写得很精辟，找不出一点毛病。

There was a man called Guo Han in the Tang Dynasty. One summer night when the moon was very bright, he suddenly saw a girl descending slowly from the sky. He observed the girl closely, and found that the dress she was wearing was seamless. He was puzzled, and asked her why that was. The girl answered, "Heavenly clothes need not be sewn with needle and thread."

This idiom is used to refer to the flawless handling of things. It can also be used to indicate a perfectly written poem or literary article.

Tóngzhōu-gòngjì

70. 同舟共济 ①

Crossing a river in the same boat

---

① 济：过河。(to cross a river)

春秋时代，吴国人和越国人经常相互打仗，成为仇敌。一次，河水泛滥，两国的人同乘一条船打算过河。船到河中间，遇到了大风，情况十分危急。两国人不分彼此，不再争斗，而是互相帮助，终于安全地渡过了河。

"同舟共济"这个成语比喻在遇到困难的时候，大家同心协力共同渡过难关。

In the Spring and Autumn Period, the State of Wu and the State of Yue often fought with each other, and their citizens looked upon each other as enemies. Once, people from the two states were crossing a river in the same boat. When the boat was in the middle of the river, a strong wind threatened to sink it. The people from the two states cooperated to ensure the safe arrival of the boat.

This idiom indicates that people should pull together to overcome difficulties, burying their differences in times of common danger.

Tōutiān-huànrì

71. 偷天換日

Stealing the sky and changing the sun

　　能够把广阔无边的天空偷走吗？能够把光芒四射的太阳换掉吗？偏偏就有那么一种人，妄想玩弄手法，偷走天空，换掉太阳。

　　"偷天换日"这个成语，用夸张的语言，比喻暗中玩弄手法，改变重大事物的真相来欺骗别人。

Can the boundless sky be stolen? Can the radiant sun be changed? There are certain people who are so keen on playing tricks that they are even dreaming to steal the sky and change the sun.

This idiom uses exaggerated words to refer to perpetrating fraud by changing important facts secretly.

Túqióng-bǐxiàn

72. 图穷匕见 ①

When the map is unrolled and the dagger is revealed

---

① 见: 同现, 表露在外面。(same as 现, being exposed)

战国末年，有一个武士荆轲受燕国太子的托付去刺杀秦王。为了能够接近秦王，荆轲便以向秦王奉献地图为名，预先把刺人的匕首藏在地图里面。秦王慢慢地展开地图，到了最后，藏在地图里的匕首就露了出来。

"图穷匕见"比喻事情发展到最后阶段，真相或本意终于暴露出来。

In the later years of the Warring States Period, Jing Ke, a warrior, was entrusted by the crown prince of the State of Yan to assassinate the ruler of the State of Qin. In order to be able to get close to the latter, Jing Ke pretended to want to present him with a valuable map in which Jing Ke had hidden a dagger. When the map was unrolled, the dagger was revealed.

This idiom means that when things come to their final stage, truth and real intentions are revealed.

Wánbì-guīzhào

73. 完璧^① 归赵

Returning the jade intact to Zhao

---

① 璧：古代的一种玉器。(a round flat piece of jade with a hole in the centre)

战国时代,秦王听说赵王有一块无价之宝"和氏璧",就写信给赵王,愿意拿十五座城来交换这块玉璧。赵王派大臣蔺相如到秦国去送玉璧。相如把玉璧献给秦王后,秦王却不打算把十五座城让给赵国。相如看破了秦王的花招,就用一个巧妙的计策把秦王骗去的玉璧弄了回来,并悄悄派人送回了赵国。

"完璧归赵"这个成语比喻借了别人的东西能够完整无损地归还给原主。

In the Warring States Period, the ruler of Qin heard that the ruler of Zhao had a piece of priceless jade. So he offered 15 cities in exchange for it. At this, the ruler of Zhao sent his minister Lin Xiangru with the jade to the State of Qin. But after Lin Xiangru presented the jade to the ruler of Qin, the ruler was not inclined to cede 15 cities to the state of Zhao and Lin Xiangru realized he had been tricked. By a ruse he managed to get the jade back, and then secretly had it sent back to his state intact.

This idiom now means returning intact what one has borrowed to its owner.

Wángyáng-bǔláo

74. 亡 ① 羊补牢 ②

Mending the fold after the sheep have been stolen

---

① 亡：丢失。(to lose)
② 牢：养牲畜的圈。(pen, fold)

从前有个人养了许多羊，有一次，他的羊圈破了一个口子，没有引起他的注意。过了几天他发现少了好几只羊，这时才后悔得不得了。邻人劝他说："羊已经丢失几只了，现在把羊圈赶快修补起来还不算晚啊！"

"亡羊补牢"这个成语比喻在受到损失以后，如果及时想办法补救，可以避免更大的损失。

A man who raised sheep once noticed that there was a hole in the wall of his sheepfold but neglected to repair it. A few days later, several sheep were missing. His neighbour advised him, "It is not too late to mend the sheepfold."

This idiom advises us that even though we have suffered a loss, it is never too late to take steps to prevent further losses.

Wàngméi-zhǐkě

75. 望梅止渴

Looking at plums to quench one's thirst

　　三国时代，有一次曹操带领军队去打仗。在行军的路上，找不到水源，士兵们都感到口渴难忍。曹操想出一个计策，指着前面一片树林说："那里就是一大片梅林，树上的梅子又甜又酸，可以解渴。"士兵们听了，想起梅子的酸味，一个个都流出了口水，再也不觉得口渴了。

　　"望梅止渴"这个成语比喻用空想来安慰自己。

In the Three Kingdoms Period, Cao Cao was once on a campaign during which his men failed to find any water. Cao Cao told them, "There are plum tress ahead. The sweet and sour plums will relieve your thirst." Hearing this, the soldiers thought of the plums and their mouths watered. This cured their thirst.

This idiom means to comfort oneself with fantasies.

Wàngyáng-xīngtàn

76. 望洋兴叹

Gazing at the ocean and sighing

有一年秋天，河里发了大水，河水淹没了田地和树林，到处都是白茫茫的一片。河神看到这种景象，自以为很伟大，很了不起。他顺着河水来到了北海，望见无边无际的海洋，水几乎和天空连在一起，这时他才感叹起来，觉得自己真是太渺小了。

"望洋兴叹"原来的意思是：看到人家的伟大，才感到自己很渺小。现在多用来比喻做事力量不够，无从着手，而感到无可奈何。

One autumn the rivers flooded, inundating a vast expanse of field and forest. Seeing this, the God of Rivers was filled with pride at his vast domain. He then journeyed to the sea. However, when he saw the mighty ocean stretching to the horizon, he realized how puny he actually was and sighed with disappointment.

This idiom originally meant feeling one's own insignificance upon seeing another's might. Now it is mostly used to indicate being able to do nothing but sigh in the face of a huge task.

Wèihǔ-zuòchāng

77. 为虎作伥

Helping the tiger to pounce upon its victims

古代有个奇怪的传说：有一只老虎把人咬死以后，它会吃掉人身上的肉，却不让人的灵魂离开。这个灵魂下次还要帮着老虎去吃人，这样的人叫伥鬼。伥鬼带着老虎去寻找第二个人，让老虎再把那个人咬死、吃掉，这时伥鬼才能够获得自由。

这个可笑的传说，后来就变成了"为虎作伥"这个成语，用来比喻替恶人做帮凶，引诱或帮助恶人干坏事。

An ancient legend has it that after a tiger ate a man, the man's soul could not be freed until it found another man for the tiger to eat.

This idiom, derived from this legend, means to do evil things in the service of the wicked.

Wòxīn-chángdǎn

78. 卧薪^① 尝胆

Sleeping on brushwood and tasting gall

---

① 薪：柴草。(brushwood)

春秋时代，越国被吴国打败了。越王勾践和他的妻子都被带到吴国做苦工。后来勾践被放回越国，他立志要报亡国之仇。从此，他每天夜里睡在柴草上面，不用被褥。在他住的地方，悬挂着一个苦胆，吃饭和睡觉以前，都要尝一尝苦胆的味道，以提醒自己不忘过去的耻辱。经过十年的艰苦奋斗，越国终于战胜了吴国。

"卧薪尝胆"这个成语用来形容刻苦自励，奋发图强。

In the Spring and Autumn Period, the State of Wu defeated the State of Yue. The Duke of Yue, Gou Jian, and his wife were sent into exile in Wu. For several years, Gou Jian labored as a slave in Wu together with his wife. When he was released and returned to Yue, Gou Jian was determined to take revenge for losing his state. He slept on a pile of brushwood and tasted gall before every meal and before he went to sleep so that he would never forget his humiliation. After ten years of careful preparations, he attacked and finally conquered the State of Wu.

This idiom is used to describe inspiring oneself and working hard to accomplish an ambition.

Xiàolǐ-cángdāo

79. 笑里藏刀

Hiding a dagger behind a smile

唐朝有一个大臣李义府，表面上对人温和恭顺，跟人谈话总是面带微笑，但是内心深处却十分阴险毒辣。凡是能力比他强的人，他都要设法加以打击和谋害。当时人们称他是"笑中刀"。

"笑里藏刀"是由"笑中刀"转化而来的，比喻表面装得善良和气，而内心暗藏阴险毒辣。

In the Tang Dynasty, there was a minister called Li Yifu who was always affable and smiling, but was in his heart very sinister and ruthless. He constantly schemed against people he saw as possible rivals and was known as "the knife in the smile".

This idiom, derived from the story, means to disguise a ruthless nature behind a pleasant appearance.

Xiōngyǒu-chéngzhú
80. 胸有成竹

Having a ready-formed plan

宋朝画家文同，特别喜欢画竹子。他在园子里种了许多竹子，经常仔细观察竹子的生长过程，特别是在晴天、雨后以及春夏秋冬不同季节里竹子的各种形态，对竹子有了较深切的了解。一旦到他提笔绘画时，他的胸中早已有了竹子的形象，所以总是能够把竹子画得生动逼真，活灵活现。

"胸有成竹"用来比喻在做事情以前，已经有了充分成熟的考虑，因而成功的把握很大。

In the Song Dynasty, an artist called Wen Tong was especially fond of drawing bamboo. He planted a lot of bamboo in his garden so that he could observe the process of their growth and appearance in different seasons and climates. He knew bamboo so well that whenever he took up the paintbrush he already had a picture in his mind, and thus he could always paint bamboo in a vivid and lively way.

This idiom means to have a well-thought-out plan in place before one sets out to do something so as to ensure its success.

Xuēzú-shìlǚ

81. 削足适履 ①

Cutting one's feet to fit one's shoes

---

① 履：鞋。(shoe)

　　汉朝有一本叫《淮南子》的书，里面叙述了一个大傻瓜的故事：傻瓜去鞋店买鞋，店主拿给他一双鞋，鞋小了，他不是让店主去换，而是打算把自己的脚削去一块，以适合鞋的大小。傻瓜去帽店买帽，帽子小了，他又打算把自己的头皮削去一点，以适合帽子的大小。

　　"削足适履"比喻办事情不顾实际情况，生搬硬套，或比喻不合理的迁就。

A book titled *Huai Nan Zi* from the Han Dynasty (206 BC-220), contains a story about a foolish man who went out to buy shoes. The shopkeeper handed him a pair that was too small. The foolish man, instead of asking for another pair, tried to cut his feet to fit the shoes. When the foolish man went to buy a cap, the first cap he tried was too small, so he tried to cut off part of his scalp so that the cap would fit.

This idiom satirizes those who handle things by rigidly applying unsuitable rules without considering the actual situation.

Yàmiáo-zhùzhǎng

82. 揠^① 苗助长

Pulling up seedlings to help them grow

---

① 揠: 拔。(to pull)

春秋时代，宋国有个急性子的种田人，庄稼长出禾苗以后，他每天都去观看，总嫌禾苗长得太慢。一天，他跑到田里去，把禾苗一棵棵往上拔。然后他很疲倦地回到家，对家里人说："今天我帮助禾苗长高了！"家里人一听，赶忙跑到田里去看，禾苗全都枯萎（wěi）了。

"揠苗助长"这个成语，现在多写成"拔苗助长"，比喻违背事物发展的客观规律，急于求成，反而把事情弄糟。

In the Spring and Autumn Period, there was a farmer who was impatient by nature. He thought his rice shoots were growing too slowly, so he decided to help them by pulling them. One day at dusk, he went back home dog-tired and said to his family, "I helped the rice shoots grow today." Hearing this, his family members hurried to the field, only to find that all the plants had withered.

This idiom is now often written as 拔苗助长. It refers to spoiling things because one is over-anxious for fast results and ignores the laws of nature.

Yǎn'ěr-dàolíng

83. 掩耳盗铃

Plugging one's ears while stealing a bell

春秋时代，晋国有一个人看中了别人的一口铜钟，想把它偷回自己家里。钟又大又重，抱不动也背不动。他脑子一转，想出一个办法：把钟砸碎，再一块一块地拿回家。于是他拿起锤子就砸。刚一砸，钟就发出"当、当、当"的响声。他怕别人听见，急忙把自己的耳朵堵了起来。这个人以为自己听不见别人也就听不见了。

"掩耳盗钟"后来变成"掩耳盗铃"，用来讽刺自作聪明、自己欺骗自己。

In the Spring and Autumn Period, a man in the State of Jin took a fancy to a bronze bell and wanted to steal it. The bell was too large and heavy to be moved, so he decided to smash it to pieces. However, when his hammer struck the bell, it made a deep booming sound. Fearing that the sound might be heard, he covered his ears and then carried on with his work. He thought that in this way nobody could hear the sound of the bell.

This idiom comes from the above story. It is used to satirize those who think they are smart but only deceive themselves.

Yǎnqí-xīgǔ

84. 偃① 旗息② 鼓

To lower the banners and silence the drums

---

① 偃：放倒。(to lay down)

② 息：停止。(to stop)

三国时代，一次曹操与刘备交战。刘备命令大将赵云、黄忠去抢夺曹操的粮食。曹操带领大军追赶赵云。赵云边打边退，一直退到营寨前，叫士兵打开营门，放倒军旗，停止擂鼓，在营外设好埋伏。曹军追到，看到这种情景，怀疑有埋伏，就撤退了。

"偃旗息鼓"这个成语现在用来比喻停止攻击或者事情中止。

In the Three Kingdoms Period, during a battle between Cao Cao and Liu Bei, the latter ordered his generals Zhao Yun and Huang Zhong to capture Cao Cao's supplies. Cao Cao led a large force against Zhao Yun, who retreated as far as the gates of his camp. There, he ordered that the banners be lowered and the war drums be silenced, and that the camp gates be left wide open. Zhao Yun then stationed his troops in ambush nearby. When Cao Cao arrived and saw the situation, he immediately suspected a trap and withdrew his forces.

This idiom is nowadays used to mean halting an attack or ceasing all activities.

Yègōng-hàolóng

85. 叶公好龙

Lord Ye loves dragons

传说古代有个叶公非常喜欢龙。他家里的墙上、柱子上、门窗上到处都画满了龙，连日常生活用的东西上也画着龙。天上的真龙知道了，非常感动，就下降到他住的地方，将头伸进窗户，尾巴拖在厅堂。叶公一见真龙，吓得脸都变了颜色，拔腿就跑。

"叶公好龙"这个成语比喻表面上爱好某种事物，但实际上并不真正爱好。或者假装爱好，实际惧怕。

In ancient times there was a Lord Ye who was very fond of dragons. In his home everything, including the walls, columns, windows, doors and even articles of daily use, were decorated with dragon designs. A real dragon was quite impressed when it heard about this, so it went to visit Lord Ye. However, when it stuck its head through the window and let its tail trail along the floor, Lord Ye was frightened and ran away.

This idiom satirizes those who profess to like or support something, but are averse to it in actual practice.

Yèláng-zìdà

86. 夜郎自大

The conceited king of Yelang

在汉朝时，西南边境上有一个小国，叫夜郎国。这个国家虽然很小，但是国王却很骄傲，自以为他的国家很大，很了不起。有一次，汉朝的使者访问夜郎国，国王问使者："汉朝与我们夜郎国比较，哪一个大呢？"

后来人们就把本来没有什么能耐却自以为很了不起而瞧不起别人，说成"夜郎自大"。

In the Han Dynasty, there was a tiny country called Yelang on the southwestern border of Han. Small though it was, its ruler was quite proud of it, thinking it big and powerful. Once, when a Han envoy visited Yelang and the ruler asked him, "Which is bigger, Han or Yelang? "

Later this idiom came to be used to refer to those who are capable of nothing yet are conceited.

Yìgǔ-zuòqì

87. 一鼓作气

Rousing the spirits with the first drum roll

春秋时代，齐国派兵攻打鲁国。鲁国的国王鲁庄公带着谋士曹刿（guì）指挥作战。齐军第一次击鼓以后，鲁军准备发起进攻。曹刿说："不行。"齐军三次击鼓以后，曹刿才说："现在可以进攻了。"结果齐军大败。战斗结束后，鲁庄公问曹刿胜利的原因。曹刿说："打仗要靠勇气。第一次击鼓，士气十分旺盛；第二次击鼓，士气有些衰落；第三次击鼓，士气就耗尽了。敌人士气耗尽，我们发起进攻，所以取得了胜利。"

后来，"一鼓作气"形容鼓起劲头，一下子把事情干完。

During the Spring and Autumn Period, an army from the State of Qi confronted one from the State of Lu. After the first roll of drums from the Qi side to summon Lu to battle, the Lu ruler wanted to attack but his counsellor Cao Gui said, "We should wait until the third drum roll." After the Qi side had beaten the drums three times, the Lu army attacked and defeated the Qi army. After the battle, the ruler of Lu asked Cao Gui the reason for his odd advice. Cao Gui answered, "Fighting needs spirit. Their spirit was roused by the first roll of the drums, but was depleted by the second and completely exhausted by the third. We started to attack when their spirit was exhausted. That's why we won."

This idiom later came to mean to get something done with one sustained effort.

Yíjiàn-shuāngdiāo

88. 一箭双雕

Killing two birds with one stone

南北朝时代，有个名叫长（zhǎng）孙晟（shèng）的人，聪明敏捷，特别善于射箭。一天他同朋友一起去打猎，忽然看见两只雕在空中争夺一块肉。他的朋友立即给了长孙晟两支箭，说："你能把两只雕都射下来吗？"长孙晟不慌不忙拉开弓，只射了一箭，就把两只雕同时射下来了。朋友直夸他好箭法。

"一箭双雕"比喻用一种方法同时得到两种收获或效果。

In the period of the Northern and Southern Dynasties there was an expert archer named Zhangsun Sheng. One day, he went hunting with a friend when suddenly they saw two vultures fighting for a piece of meat high in the air. His friend handed him two arrows and said, "Can you shoot down both vultures?" Zhangsun Sheng effortlessly killed both vultures with only one arrow.

This idiom means to achieve two things at a single stroke.

Yìmíng-jīngrén

89. 一鸣惊人

Amazing the world with a single feat

战国时代，齐威王即位后做了三年国君，只顾享乐，不理政事。有个善于说笑话的人叫淳（chún）于髡（kūn），一天他对齐威王说："城里有一只大鸟，三年不飞也不叫，你知道这是什么道理？"齐威王说："这鸟不飞则罢，一飞就冲天；不鸣则罢，一鸣就惊人。"在淳于髡的激发下，齐威王开始治理国家，取得很大成绩，齐国的声威一直保持了几十年。

"一鸣惊人"用来表示平时默默无闻，一旦行动起来，却做出惊人的成绩。

In the Warring States Period, Duke Wei of Qi neglected state affairs for the first three years of his reign, instead giving himself over to dissipation. One of his ministers, Chun Yukun who had a good sense of humour, said to him, "There is a large bird which has neither taken wing nor sung for three years. Do you know the reason for this?" The duke answered, "Once that bird starts to fly and sing, it will astonish the world." Henceforth the duke devoted himself to his duties and built his state into a powerful one.

This idiom is used to indicate that a person may rise from obscurity and achieve greatness.

Yìqiū-zhīhé

90. 一丘之貉 ①

Jackals of the same lair

---

① 貉：一种哺乳动物。(racoon dog)

汉朝时，有个叫杨恽（yùn）的人，在朝廷做官，廉洁无私，又很有才能。有一次，他听说一个小国王被杀死，就发表议论说："君王不采纳贤臣的计策，就会得到这种下场。秦朝皇帝宠信奸臣，所以亡国；如果重用贤臣，他的国家就不会亡了。"他最后总结说，古今的帝王都不过是一个山丘上的貉而已。

"一丘之貉"这个成语比喻某些人彼此相同，或者都是坏人。

In the Han Dynasty, there was an official called Yang Yun who was both capable and honest. Commenting on the assassination of the king of a small state, he said, "If a king refuses to follow the advice of a wise minister, he will suffer an untimely death. The emperor of the Qin Dynasty trusted treacherous ministers, and therefore lost his state." He then compared kings and emperors to racoon dogs living on the same mountain.

This idiom refers derogatorily to people who are of the same kind.

Yúgōng-yíshān

91. 愚公移山

The foolish old man who removed the mountains

古代有个愚公，他家门前有两座大山挡住去路，出门很不方便。愚公决心率领他的子孙们挖掉这两座大山。有个智叟劝阻他说："你太傻了。像你这么大年纪，连小山都平不了，还想搬走两座大山？"愚公笑笑说："我死了有儿子，儿子死了有孙子，子子孙孙无穷无尽，而山不会增高了，还愁把它挖不平？"愚公的精神感动了天帝，于是天帝派了两个神仙把两座山搬走了。

"愚公移山"比喻做事有顽强的毅力，不怕困难，坚持到底。

In ancient times, there was an old man in front of whose house were two high mountains which made it very inconvenient for him to come and go. He gathered his family and started to level the mountains. His neighbour scoffed, "You are foolish. You are too old and weak to level a small hill, let alone two big mountains." However, the old man said, "I have sons, and my sons have sons. I will have endless progeny, but the mountains won't grow any higher." The spirit of the "Foolish Old Man" moved Heaven, and so it sent two immortals to move the mountains away.

This idiom describes an indomitable will.

Yúmù-hùnzhū

92. 鱼目混珠

Passing off fish eyes as pearls

汉朝时候有个叫魏伯阳的人，写了一本讲述道家炼丹的书。在这本书里有两句很有意思的话："鱼目怎么能混同于珍珠，蓬蒿（pénghāo）绝不能冒充茶树。"鱼的眼睛和珍珠看起来有点相像，但是价值就大不相同了。

"鱼目混珠"这个成语，比喻用假的东西冒充真的东西。

In the Han Dynasty, there was a Taoist called Wei Boyang who wrote a book on the making of pills of immortality. In this book there was the following line, "Fish eyes can't be passed off as pearls, and bitter fleabane can't pretend to be a tea plant." Fish eyes may look like pearls, but they are valueless.

This idiom is used to mean passing off something false as being genuine.

Yúyīn-ràoliáng
93. 余音绕梁

The tune lingers in the house

　　战国时候，韩国有个女子名叫韩娥。她的嗓音很好，唱起歌来，美妙动听。有一次她出门经过齐国，粮食吃完了，只好靠卖唱来维持生活。不久之后，韩娥离开了齐国，可是她的歌声却还回荡在人们的屋梁附近，一直过了三天都没有消失。齐国的人们都以为韩娥还没有走呢。

　　"余音绕梁"这个成语用来形容歌声优美，使人很久不能忘怀。

In the Warring States Period, there was a girl in the State of Han called Han Eh who sang beautifully. Once, when she was passing through the State of Qi, she had to sing to earn money to buy food. When she left Qi, the echoes of her songs clung to the beams of the houses there for three days before people realized that she had left.

This idiom is used to describe unforgettably beautiful singing.

Yǔhǔ-móupí

94. 与虎谋皮

Borrowing the skin from a tiger

　　传说古代有个人非常爱好皮衣和珍异的美味。他想做一件价值千金的皮衣，就去跟狐狸商量要它的皮。他想吃鲜美的羊肉，就去跟羊商量要它的肉。狐狸和羊听见他说这样的话，都逃到远远的地方去了。

　　这个故事原来叫"与狐谋皮"，后来转化成"与虎谋皮"，比喻跟恶人商量要他牺牲自己的利益，那是绝对办不到的。

In ancient times, there was a man who was very fond of fur clothes and fine food. He asked a fox to give him its pelt, but the fox ran away. He then asked a sheep for its meat, but the sheep too ran away.

与狐谋皮, later known as 与虎谋皮, means that it is impossible to discuss with the vicious the possibility of gaining profits from them.

Yùbàng-xiāngzhēng

95. 鹬 ① 蚌 ② 相争

A snipe and a clam locked in combat

---

① 鹬：吃鱼类、贝类的鸟。(snipe)

② 蚌：带壳的软体动物。(clam)

　　一只河蚌张开了壳，在河滩上晒太阳。忽然一只鹬猛地把尖尖的嘴伸过来啄蚌的肉。蚌立刻合拢它的壳，紧紧地夹住了鹬的嘴。鹬说："今天不下雨，明天不下雨，你就会被太阳晒死！"蚌说："你的嘴今天不出来，明天不出来，你就会饿死！"双方互不相让，正巧走过来一个渔夫，就把它们一同捉走了。

　　"鹬蚌相争"比喻双方相持不下，两败俱伤，让第三者得到了好处。

　　One day a clam opened its shell to sunbathe on a beach. Suddenly a snipe stuck its beak in the clam. The latter closed its shell immediately, and trapped the snipe's beak. The clam refused to open its shell, and the snipe refused to remove its beak. The snipe said, "If it doesn't rain today or tomorrow, you will be burnt to death by the sun." The clam replied, "If you refuse to remove your beak today or tomorrow, you will starve to death." Neither of them would compromise. Finally, a fisherman came along and caught both of them.

　　This idiom means that if two sides contend, it will be a third party that ultimately benefits.

Zhāosān-mùsì

96. 朝三暮四

Three in the morning and four in the evening

　　春秋时代，宋国有一个人，养了一大群猴子。这些猴子能够听懂主人说的话。过了一段时间，主人家里穷了，想限制一下猴子每天吃的粮食。于是他对猴子说:"每天给你们吃的橡（xiàng）子，早上三个，晚上四个，够了吗？"猴子们听了，都怒气冲冲地站了起来。主人又说:"早上四个，晚上三个，够了吗？"猴子们听了，都趴（pā）在地上表示满意。

　　"朝三暮四"原来表示欺骗和愚弄的手段，以后改用来比喻说话、做事反复无常。

In the Spring and Autumn Period, a man in the State of Song raised monkeys who could understand what he said. As the man became poor, he wanted to reduce the monkeys' amount of food. He first suggested that he give them four acorns in the morning and three acorns in the evening. Upon hearing this, the monkeys protested angrily. Their owner then said, "How about three in the morning and four in the evening?" The monkeys were satisfied with that.

This idiom originally meant to befool others with tricks. Later it came to mean to keep changing one's mind.

Zhǐgāo-qìyáng

97. 趾^① 高气扬

Stepping high and haughtily

---

① 趾：脚。(Foot)

春秋时代，楚国出兵攻打罗国。一个名叫斗伯比的官员去送行，他看到带兵的主帅的样子，回来后私下对人说："这次出征，主帅走路时脚抬得高高的，一副神气十足、傲慢轻敌的样子。这样恐怕是要打败仗的！"果然不出所料，这次战斗，楚国大败，连主帅也自杀了。

"趾高气扬"这个成语用来形容骄傲自满、得意忘形。

In the Spring and Autumn Period, the State of Chu sent troops to attack the State of Luo. An official called Dou Bobi went to see the troops off. When he came back, he said to someone secretly, "The general walked in an arrogant way, he was stepping high. I'm afraid he will be defeated." Sure enough, the Chu troops were badly defeated, and the general committed suicide.

This idiom is used to describe being arrogant and putting on airs.

Zhǐlù-wéimǎ

98. 指鹿为马

Calling a stag a horse

秦朝丞相赵高想篡（cuàn）夺皇位，怕群臣
们不服气，就想了一个办法来试一试大家。他牵
来一只鹿献给皇帝说："这是一匹马。"皇帝笑着说：
"丞相你弄错了吧？这是一只鹿。"赵高就问旁边
的大臣们。他们有的不做声，有的跟着赵高说是
马，也有说是鹿的。凡是说鹿的人，后来都被赵
高杀了。从此以后，群臣都害怕赵高。

"指鹿为马"用来比喻故意颠倒黑白，混淆
（xiáo）是非。

In the Qin Dynasty, the prime minister, Zhao Gao,
plotted to overthrow the emperor. Fearing that the other
ministers would oppose this, he thought of a way of testing
them. He presented a deer to the emperor, and said, "This is a
horse." The emperor laughed and said, "You must be joking;
this is a deer." Then Zhao Gao asked the same quesiton to the
ministers present. Some kept silent, some said that it was a
deer, and others agreed that it was a horse.

Later Zhao Gao had all the ministers who had not said
that it was a horse killed.

This metaphor describes distorting facts by calling white
black and vice versa.

Zhǐshàng-tánbīng
99. 纸上谈兵 ①

Discussing strategems on paper

———————

① 兵：兵法，兵书。(the art of war; book on the art of war)

战国时，赵国名将赵奢 (shē) 的儿子赵括喜欢看书、谈兵法。他把兵书背得滚瓜烂熟，谈起打仗来头头是道，似乎他的父亲也比不过他。一次秦国攻打赵国，赵王派赵括率领四十万大军去抵抗。由于他只知道死抠书本而不会在实际中灵活运用，最后指挥失策，以致全军覆没，他自己也中箭身亡。

后来人们根据这一历史故事，把死抠书本、没有实践经验、只会夸夸其谈称为"纸上谈兵"。

In the Warring States Period, the State of Zhao had a famous general called Zhao She, whose son, Zhao Kuo, was very fond of reading books on military science and discussing military strategy. He could recite military texts by heart, and when discussing warfare, he spoke so clearly and logically that it seemed that even his father could not match for his talents. So when the State of Qin attacked the State of Zhao, the ruler of Zhao ordered Zhao Kuo to lead 400,000 men to repel the attack. However, despite all his knowledge, Zhao Kuo had no practical experience of battle, so he was defeated and lost his life.

Later, people began to use this idiom to describe those who are good at theorizing but lack practical experience.

Zìxiāng-máodùn

100. 自相矛盾

Contradicting oneself

古代有个卖矛和盾的人。他一手举起他的矛夸耀说:"我的矛锋利无比,无论多么坚硬的东西都能刺穿。"过了一会儿,他又举起另一只手里的盾说:"我的盾坚硬无比,无论多么锋利的东西也刺不破。"观众中有一个人问他:"用你的矛刺你的盾,结果会怎样呢?"这个人被问得哑口无言了。

"自相矛盾"用来比喻说话或做事不一致,互相抵触。

In ancient times, there was a man who sold spears and shields. He used to boast, "My spears are the sharpest things in the world. They can penetrate anything." A moment later he would boast, "My shields are the toughest things in the world. Nothing can penetrate them." One day, a passer-by asked him, "What would happen if you threw one of your spears at one of your shields?"

This idiom is used metaphorically to refer to contradictions in one's own speech or action.

Zuòjiǎn-zìfù

101. 作茧自缚

Spinning a cocoon around oneself

蚕吐丝作茧时，把自己包在里面。

"作茧自缚"比喻人做事原来希望于自己有利，结果却反使自己吃亏受到连累。也比喻自己束缚自己。

The silkworm produces silk to cocoon itself.

The idiom is metaphorically used to mean that someone intends to benefit himself by doing sth., which actually ends up backfiring on them, and the idiom also refers to restraining oneself.